Marketing Mindset

The Ultimate Guide to Positioning Yourself as the Go-To Expert in Your Niche

By Mark E. Klipsch

Marketing Mindset

ISBN 978-0-692-37331-6

Published in the United States of America
by MEKA Multicast Marketing
5640-B Telegraph Road, Suite 159
St. Louis, MO 63129

Acknowledgements

This book was written because of my passion for business. Since I was young I've been intrigued by business and the sales process. I've been a keen student, made many mistakes along the way, and been blessed to find some successes. I'm forever grateful to my family, friends, mentors and clients for the support, patience and guidance you've given me.

Dan and Amy Klipsch, my incredible children, I am always inspired by the people you've grown to be. My family – Mom, Dad, Patty, Joyce and Ron – you have always been there and are a reminder of the unconditional love of family. My aunts, uncles, grandparents and great-grandparents, while some of you have passed on from this world; you have been terrific role models in my life. I can't express my gratitude for all that you've taught me.

My mastermind brothers and sisters – thank you for pushing me to get this project done. This book wouldn't have been completed without your support and encouragement.

My mentors; Dan Kennedy, Mike Koenigs, Frank Kern and so many others – thank you for guiding me with your knowledge, expertise and wisdom.

Finally, my customers and clients both past and present; it's been a pleasure and a privilege serving you. Without you, there would be no business. Thank you for trusting me and believing in me. You continue to be my inspiration.

Table of Contents

Acknowledgements iv

Introduction 1

Section I: Mindset: What is Marketing?   **9**

Chapter One: Target the Right Market. 13

Chapter Two: Create a Compelling Message 25

Chapter Three: Select the Right Media 35

Chapter Four: Measure and Manage for Success . . .47

Section II: Positioning: Your Platform is Your Greatest Asset   **59**

Chapter Five: Position Yourself as Expert. 61

Chapter Six: Get Published 69

Chapter Seven: Promote and Profit 81

Section III: Formula: Wash, Rinse and Repeat   **89**

Chapter Eight: Build a Powerful, Repeatable Method 91

Chapter Nine: Execute It Again and Again 107

Additional Resources 115

About the Author. 119

Introduction

The purpose of this book is to help you, the small business person, rise to the top of your niche in terms of position, sales, reputation and expertise. Perhaps you've already experienced some successes, yet still can't help wondering why connecting with customers, clients or patients can be so difficult.

When you begin to incorporate the strategies I'm going to share with you throughout this book, you'll become magnetic to your IDEAL customer, easily attracting them to you like a moth to bright light. Just as importantly, you'll discover those less-than-ideal clients will stop beating a path to your door.

These strategies will result in a much easier and more efficient sales process when executed properly. In turn, you will find your business in greater demand and be able to increase your fees and prices, leaving your competitors stumped.

What you're about to discover will help position you to become the expert in your marketplace. The best part is that you'll be delivering a great customer experience before the sale ever occurs. Not only will your prospects thank you, they will become customers who will trust you, refer you and reward you with their business for years to come.

I've broken this book into three sections: Mindset, Positioning and Formula. This corresponds to the knowledge I've gained from the three mentors to whom I credit the majority of my success and thinking regarding business development and marketing: Dan Kennedy, Mike Koenigs and Frank Kern.

Before I jump into how you can grow your business with the right marketing mindset, I want to take a moment to introduce myself. I believe it's important for you to read a bit of my story so you understand a little about me, my entrepreneurial journey and how I ended up a small business consultant.

My story actually begins with my great grandfather. In the early twentieth century, coal was the primary method for heating indoor spaces. In 1926, seeing an opportunity, he began hauling coal from the mines in southern Illinois into St. Louis, Missouri and selling it to home and business owners. His business thrived, but other forms of heating began to replace coal, which meant the business had to evolve – or die. My grandfather, father and uncles transformed the Klipsch & Sons Coal Co. business into the Klipsch Hauling Co., a successful tank truck business, which was acquired by a competitor in the early 1980s.

The entrepreneurial spirit runs deep in my family. In high school, I began cutting lawns and doing small landscape projects as Klipsch Estate Management. I learned to market, sell and deliver on the agreements I made with home and business owners. The lessons I learned proved invaluable as I made my own mark in trucking and other businesses. I'll share some of those stories in the coming chapters.

The family business was sold to a competitor in the early eighties, shortly after my entry into it. My father, uncles and I continued working for the new company in various roles. In my first assignment, I was asked to take on a temporary management role in Memphis, Tennessee. The company had just terminated the facility manager, so I was to handle day-to-day operations until new personnel were hired. Can you imagine, as a twenty-something kid, I was going to a new city charged with managing a group of truck drivers and other personnel all of whom were ten to thirty years older than I was. They knew I was green as the grass and questioned my every decision. It taught me quickly to be prepared to explain my reasoning and defend my choices. I stayed focused my job and, within 90 days, I turned over the reins to new management. Since then, I've often joked that I spent a year in Memphis one summer.

Soon after, I was given a new opportunity. The company had never been able to break into the Chicago market but with deregulation of the trucking industry now firmly in place, the marketplace was open to new competition. Two colleagues and I leased space, began calling on potential clients, and within a year had outgrown our office space and moved the business to what would become its permanent home. The company's Chicago operations are still running from this same location now thirty years later. In those early years though, we struggled like every new business trying to find our niche, hire the right people and build the systems that would support our growth objectives. Long hours, heated debates, demanding customers and cold, harsh Chicago winters challenged us at every turn. I stayed with the company for five years before being recruited by another tank truck firm to start up a new business for them in another new market.

Over the next seven and a half years, I not only helped this new company create a business, but also started another in the construction industry and helped guide the turn-around of three other companies. In each case, I worked about eighteen months to implement my systems and build a stable base of business before moving on to the next opportunity. To be clear, I made mistakes. I learned to fail fast, absorb new information quickly and keep moving forward. During this time, I married, fathered two great children and completed my bachelor's degree. Armed with a family, some formal education and a track record of success, I decided I wanted more. I'd become sought after as the startup/turnaround expert for transport companies looking to expand into new territory or for help with struggling businesses. If I was going to continue to build businesses for other people, I decided that I wanted more than just a salary for my blood, sweat and tears. When the owner of the last trucking company I'd been working with turned down my request for a piece of his company, I reasoned that it was time to start my own.

My father strenuously counseled me against this decision, but in 1994, I started RMC Intermodal Services. I recognized an opportunity in the market; a growing demand for liquid bulk transport on an international level. I reached out to one of the industry leaders of the day who was building his company by supporting small domestic tank truck operators around the country through an affiliation model, similar to a franchise business model. While the leader of this organization admittedly didn't really understand the opportunity in the international market that I was eager to pursue, he welcomed it and supported me fully. Eleven years later, I'd grown my business to a respectable $10 million in annual revenue, a fleet of nearly forty trucks, and more than fifty employees. It was at times a lot of fun, always grueling, and often rewarding, but at age 41, I found myself undergoing a cardiac catheterization procedure. It was the wake-up call I didn't know I needed! I realized some changes were needed in my life, or I might not see my children graduate from high school, much less enjoy anything else in life. A year later, in 2006, I sold my business and began to look for new opportunities. I knew the marketing and business development strategies I'd been employing for the past twenty-five years were formulaic, which meant I expected to see similar results regardless of the industry to which the strategies were applied. I was anxious to execute them in other industries to see if I truly would achieve similar positive business outcomes.

I'm happy to report that the formula works. I've applied it to the development of businesses in insurance, financial services, medical technology, consumer services, construction, package engineering and wholesale distribution. In all, I've had the opportunity to be involved in the start-up or turnaround twenty-three different businesses in a variety of industries over a thirty-five-year career.

I'm excited to share the lessons I've learned. My hope is that you, too, will successfully implement them in your business. I'd like to hear your success stories, so I've created a Facebook page to give you a forum, "Marketing Mindset Book." Please join so you can learn from me and other business owners as well as share your questions, suggestions and successes.

Let's get started!

Section I:
Mindset:
What is Marketing?

Congratulations! Just by getting to this first chapter, you're already ahead of your competition because most people don't take the actions necessary for success. You've gotten this far, now let's go the rest of the way together.

Before we get into specific strategies, it's important that we review some basic principles and the mindset needed for effective marketing. Let's start by answering the question "What is Marketing?" This question has been answered many different ways; however, my favorite answer comes from one of the most provocative, irreverent and no B.S. guys in the business, Dan Kennedy.

Dan S. Kennedy started in the advertising business in the early 1970s at a young age with no academic credentials, formal training or apprenticeship. In the forty years since, he has advised Fortune 500 and major brand name corporations worldwide as well as thousands of entrepreneurs and small business owners on the nuances of effective marketing. A sought-after speaker, Dan has presented on stages all over the United States and written numerous books that have been featured in Success and Entrepreneur Magazines and many others. You can find his books everywhere including Amazon.com.

Dan's been one of my mentors for over twenty years. He defines marketing as:

"Getting the Right Message, to the Right Market, via the Right Media and Methods, effectively, efficiently, and profitably."

This translates into a handy triangle illustration.

Marketing Results Triangle

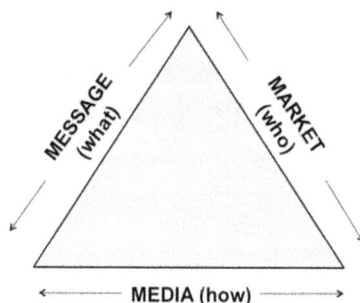

To get the most out of your marketing, you need an effective mix – and it's not all about the media. You may prefer to think of it like a three-legged stool. If a three-legged stool has only two legs, there's no way that stool can stand up for long. The same is true in marketing. You need all three legs for your marketing to stand. If you get any one of them wrong, your business will be wobbly at best and completely ineffectual at worst. You'll probably waste a lot of money before you figure that out.

When you look at most of the advertising and marketing that's generated today, perhaps even your own, it's usually the media side that receives the greatest amount of attention, with the cheapest options used the most. Is it any wonder that so many business owners fret daily about their customers being so price sensitive, when they themselves approach their marketing asking the question, "How cheaply can I get a new customer?"

So where should you begin?

Chapter One:
Target the Right Market

One of the trucking clients I worked with years ago was struggling mightily to stay afloat. While the company had been in business nearly six years, it was lucky to break even each year after paying debts on its equipment. Marty, the owner, was exhausted. After six long years with no vacations, logging sixty to seventy-hour weeks and struggling with a fleet of worn out trucks, he was ready to give up. He was seriously considering closing up shop and working for someone else. Fortunately, one of Marty's customers knew me from work I'd done with another company's turnaround and made the introduction. Soon after, I began helping Marty save his company.

Most business owners never give thought to who their ideal customers are or how to attract them. Marty was no exception. He had started his company by accumulating information about competing companies, including learning their customer lists and pricing. With this data in hand, he began calling on potential customers offering them competitive pricing. For six long years, he built his company on the belief that he could discount his competitors' prices by a couple of points and win the business. His strategy worked; he won a reasonable number of accounts.

His strategy was well-reasoned but misguided. His biggest mistake was assuming his competitors were smart and profitable. In reality, his competition was no smarter than he was. This strategy, discounting against competitors' rates, is so common it's scary. I see the blind leading the blind in all industries. Truthfully, competing on price alone is horrible business strategy.

Marty made another mistake by trying to be "all things to all customers." If one wanted him to haul a load of product from Chicago to Dallas, Marty did his best to accommodate. If another customer wanted him to haul a load to New York, he did. The problem is that unless you're operating a fleet of trucks the size of United Parcel Service, there's no way to operate that business efficiently. It would be that same problem for a local home cleaning service with one vehicle attempting to clean several homes daily but accepting customers at random spread over an entire metropolitan area.

The good news for Marty was that his problems were not insurmountable. He didn't have to walk away from the business he'd built, but he did need to revise his thinking…a lot. We began by analyzing his business and existing customers looking for commonality in service needs and territories. We identified a sufficient need among his existing customers for trucking services along the Interstate 80 corridor between Chicago and New Jersey, which would eliminate the randomness of route assignments. Even better, we identified many other potential customers along this same route. Next, we properly assessed his costs for providing service on this route and created a sensible, profit-promoting price strategy. Within eighteen months of purposefully prospecting and choosing his IDEAL customers using this new strategy, he was able to increase pricing by 300 percent, achieve a customer service rating of ninety-seven percent, replace the existing fleet of old trucks, grow the total fleet by four times and turn the company into a business Marty was proud to own.

A few years later, Marty sold his company to a member of his management team. The company is still operating today, and has continued to grow by following the formula for identifying and cultivating its IDEAL customers.

Who are you attracting to your business? Who is your IDEAL customer?

You cannot begin to address your message or media until you know whom you want to attract. Here are six key questions you should be able to answer about your target market.

1. What is their passion or desire in life? What do they want?
2. What gets in the way of getting what they want?
3. Whom do they love?
4. Whom do they hate?
5. What do they love?
6. What do they hate?

These questions get at the heart of who they are. They pinpoint the issues that keep customers and prospects up at night. They identify whom they enjoy spending time with and whom they wish could be extricated from their lives. These questions provide valuable information on how they spend their leisure time and what things they would rather do without in their life. These questions help you "go deep" with prospects and current clients to determine how you might best help them or not.

Here is an brief example of how much information you can get about a prospect or client.

We'll start with Mike. Mike is in his forties, and been married for about fifteen years to his college sweetheart. They have two beautiful children who are in private school and participate in numerous athletic and artistic activities. Mike owns a local painting contractor business where he supervises a dozen or so painters. He also functions as the salesperson and project planner. Mike's wife keeps the books, handles payroll, billing and any other administrative work that needs to be done. They attend a Christian church in their community and are active in their children's school and activities. Mike enjoys hunting, fishing, playing golf and the outdoors. His wife and children also enjoy the outdoors and spend time camping, boating, snowmobiling and skiing together. Mike leans right politically, supports the second amendment and would like less government intervention in his life. Mike's greatest concern is being able to continue providing for his family, plan a secure retirement and have time for the things he enjoys given the current economy and uncertainty about the future.

Down the street from Mike lives Steve. Like Mike, Steve is also married and has two children. Steve's children attend the local public school and participate in school sponsored athletic and artistic activities. Steve is the plant manager of a large manufacturing company and his wife works part-time at a local retail store to help pay the bills. Steve's company has been downsizing and, while he's worked there for 15 years, he's recently become unsure about his future. Steve has a timeshare

17

vacation rental at Disney in Orlando, Florida, where they try to escape for two weeks each summer. Steve leans far more left than Mike, but he wouldn't call himself a liberal. He does support the idea of gun control, and believes that community college should be free to attend like K-12 public education. He believes that government intervention is the best way to improve our community, because greedy corporate entities, like his employer, don't do enough to support the community or their employees. Steve's greatest concern is being able to continue providing for his family, plan a secure retirement and have time for the things he enjoys given the current economy and uncertainty about his future.

Knowing this much about my clients enables me to attract others like Mike or Steve. With this information, I can now write a marketing message that speaks to them in terms that will resonate with each of them and cause them to respond. A message aimed to attract clients like Mike would likely include politically conservative topics dealing with healthcare reform, gun ownership rights and reference current hot button topics such as personal responsibility. Delivering that same message to Steve, however, would be repelling to him. Additionally, I search for the media where my message will most likely reach Mike; conservative radio and TV programs, sportsman's magazines and journals, and media outlets popularized by conservative celebrities. If Steve happens to listen or watch those shows, or pick up such a magazine, even if he's interested in the product or service being offered, the message delivered won't resonate.

Sadly, many business owners can't readily describe whom it is they want to attract, nor can they describe their current customers with any degree of accuracy. It's quite probable they've never given a moment's thought to who their IDEAL client might be. Is it any wonder they're continually frustrated in their business?

While it's possible to attract both Mike and Steve to your business, you'll be far more successful if you take the time to understand their differences and design marketing messages that will resonate with them personally and place these messages in media they are most likely to see.

If you've been in business for any length of time and have a variety of customers, clients or patients, then I suggest you start by asking this one question:

> Who is my BEST client? Who is the client that, when you think about them you could say, "Gee, if ALL of my clients looked like Joe, wouldn't my business be more fun, less work and more profitable?"

Marketing Mindset

Once you've identified this client or clients (you can have more than one BEST client), then answer the six questions I listed previously for each one:

1. What is their passion or desire in life? What do they want?
2. What gets in the way of getting what they want?
3. Whom do they love?
4. Whom do they hate?
5. What do they love?
6. What do they hate?

It's also a great idea for you take a few minutes to answer these questions yourself. See how your answers compare to those of your BEST clients. Don't be surprised if you see some commonality between your answers and each of your clients. It's no secret that people like to do business with those most like themselves.

If you're just starting out in business and don't have many (or any) clients yet, this exercise is still valuable. Knowing that your BEST clients are likely to have much in common with you, you'll want to use that information to attract the right clients at the start of your new business.

Chapter One: Target the Right Market

Understanding your IDEAL client is the first step toward moving your business in a successful direction.

Chapter Summary

While it's great you believe that your products and services can benefit everyone, you don't have the time or resources to market to the entire world, even if the entire world needs your stuff. Your business will be much more successful and grow much faster when you narrow your audience and get clear about whom your IDEAL client is.

Below are some additional questions you may want to begin asking:

- Who are you best customers?
- Where do they live?
- What are their occupations?
- What's their education level?
- What is their age range?
- Are they male or female?
- What's their marital status?
- Do they have children?
  o   What are the age ranges of the children?
- Do they own their home or rent?
- What's their income level?
- What is their political affiliation?
- What are their lifestyle preferences?

- o   Do they play golf? Bike? Hike? Run?
- o   Do they travel/vacation? Where?
- o   Are they investors?
  - ▪   Stocks?
  - ▪   Bonds?
  - ▪   Real Estate?
- Do they have a religious affiliation?
- Are they philanthropically minded?
  - o   What types of causes do they support?
    - ▪   Community based?
    - ▪   Humanitarian?
    - ▪   Environmental?
    - ▪   Healthcare?
    - ▪   Animal?
- What do they read?
  - o   Books?
  - o   Magazines?
- What are their likes? Dislikes?
- Are they members of civic or professional organizations, associations or group?
- What do they value from your company, products or services?
- What do they ask for, or what do they want from your current products/services that you don't currently offer?

Marketing Mindset

This is not intended to be a complete or exhaustive list by any means, but instead a starting point. The better you know your IDEAL client, the easier it becomes to attract them to your offering.

Chapter Two:
Create a Compelling Message

Attracting your IDEAL clients, customers or patients is a lot like fishing. Now I realize that not everyone who reads this book enjoys fishing as much as I do, but stick with me for a moment.

Doesn't it make sense that the bait you choose will attract some fish and repel others? I hope so, and if not, please trust me when I tell you that when I'm fishing for crappie or bass, a worm will probably do the job. If I'm fishing for salmon on Lake Michigan, the worm's not likely to get attention. Dan Kennedy always says, "Match the Bait to the Critter."

Creating a message that speaks to your IDEAL customer works much the same way. Using the same six questions that you answered about your IDEAL customer and yourself, you can create a message that addresses one or more of those issues. This message will be attention getting and attractive to your IDEAL customer. But don't miss my point here – it's not all about the customer. By revealing some things about yourself in your messaging, you become relatable to your prospect or client. Including personal stories or information is like supercharging a magnet.

Most advertising and marketing messages are a tremendous waste. They are often unclear and unfocused. They get poor results because they put out no bait, that is, they use ordinary imagery or brand advertising. Sometimes they just use lousy bait. For example, ads that list a menu of services make it difficult for the prospect to know if the advertiser can actually solve his problem.

Confused prospects will not take action!

The lesson here is not to copy big corporations that are only creating brand awareness. Building a brand is fine once you have thousands of customers coming in the door. Until then, you can't afford it. You need buyers NOW!

A client in the wholesale lighting business had this very problem. He needed customers...yesterday! Ken's company represented the leading manufacturer of general illumination LED lighting products. The brand is known for its quality and value.

After reviewing Ken's sales data, we determined that Ken's best prospects were building owners and maintenance engineers who had already begun upgrading their facilities with LED lighting but were frustrated with the poor quality of the products flooding the market. Ken knew that he had a great solution to their big problem, a quality product backed up with an industry leading warranty and a value proposition that created an ROI for his buyer in twelve to sixteen months. For Ken, getting customers to buy wasn't really the problem; it was finding those frustrated building owners and maintenance engineers who were seeking his solution.

We crafted a message that spoke directly to their frustration and targeted the building owners and maintenance engineers in geographic territories with significant density. By targeting in this way, we believed that even if our message didn't reach our prospects directly, we would benefit from their close proximity and likelihood of sharing information. Since this is an ongoing campaign, I'm not at liberty to share specific results. However, I can share that Ken's lead generation rate is currently running about eight to ten percent.

There are five key elements of a good marketing message that when used together will dramatically increase its effectiveness:

1. Clearly articulate the problem
2. Offer a solution

3. Create urgency to elicit a response
4. Provide clear instructions
5. Track and measure results

Successful entrepreneurs are problem solvers. Your customers and prospects don't care about your credentials, how long you've been in business or how many accolades you've received. They care about one thing and one thing only – can you solve their problem?

Your message, therefore, must absolutely address their PROBLEM. The better you understand their problem and the pain they're in and build your message around that, the more likely they are to see you as empathetic. Only when they know that you can feel their pain, and accurately diagnose that pain, will they be receptive to your prescription or solution.

So buy all means, offer them a SOLUTION! Ask for the order! The late author and speaker Zig Ziglar used to say, "Timid salesmen have skinny kids." He means that whether your message is delivered nose-to-nose through a salesperson or through a marketing piece, if you don't make an offer you won't make a sale.

I don't often see marketing that does a good job of articulating a problem, and even when I have, there's seldom an offer. Let's take that one step further and say, if you're going to make an offer, make it an irresistible offer. If you truly believe that your solution can help people, don't you have a moral obligation to present it?

I realize that not every company is in the business of offering life-changing solutions, so moral obligation may be a bit strong, but please understand that you must make an offer.

The third key element is URGENCY. Along with offering a solution, you need to create some urgency, a reason that they must act…This Week…Today…Now! What will it take to move someone to action from inaction? Your message must also provide CLEAR INSTRUCTIONS as to what you want them to do. This is too important to leave to chance. As I stated earlier, a confused client or prospect does NOT act. It might seem silly to you, but I've seen response rates increase when the only change to a message was from "Call 321-555-1212" to "Call Now to Get Your Free Report 321-555-1212."

Finally, there must be TRACKING and MEASUREMENT. In the next chapter, we're going to talk about media, including what works, and how many types to utilize. It's important to recognize that when you are running multiple campaigns simultaneously using a variety of media, you're going to need to build tracking and measurement mechanisms into your message so you can manage each campaign. You need to know what works and what doesn't as well as tracking your return on investment for each campaign. You simply can't rely upon asking prospects how they heard about you, it's too subjective and people have faulty memories.

You'll discover that some campaigns will work better than others will. Some may provide fantastic ROI while others just breakeven or worse. By the way, breakeven isn't necessarily bad depending upon the lifetime value of your customer. We'll talk about that later in the book. For now, just understand that you can't manage what you don't measure. When it comes to investing in marketing and advertising, you want to know what kind of return you're getting. You wouldn't hand your retirement account to a financial advisor without requiring a precise accounting of its status, and you shouldn't invest in marketing and advertising without similar expectations.

One last thought on messaging. I mentioned earlier the concept of revealing a bit of you in the message. There are numerous ways to apply this strategy, and before we move on to talk about media, I want to leave you with two ideas to consider.

Create affinity. In what organizations are you a member? What social, healthcare, political or religious causes do you support? When you reveal this kind of information in your messaging, people will respond because they will feel that "you're just like they are" and they'll want to do business with you.

In my community, there is a furniture store that has successfully added a PSA (public service announcement) to every advertisement. In the PSA, they encourage the spaying and neutering of household pets. This resonates with the people in the community who love their pets, hate "puppy mills" and the over-population of unwanted pets that leads to euthanizing. Because this furniture store supports and gives attention to a problem that touches the hearts and souls of the community, the community responds by rewarding them with their business. In fact, one of their former competitors just went out of business. Affinity matters.

Get personal. What's important in your life? Young children, aging parents, travel, recreation? Tell short stories about your latest vacation experience, your child's first hit in little league ball or the challenges of caring for an aging parent. It lets people know you're real, and not just some cold nameless business trying to get a hand in their checkbook.

When you incorporate short stories about what's important to you in your messaging, others will be inspired to share their stories with you. You'll get letters or posts in blog and social media spaces from prospects and clients telling their stories about similar experiences. People you've never met will approach you as if they've known you forever because you've shared something in which they can relate.

Now that you've created a great message that speaks to your IDEAL client's pain, positions you as the expert, prescribes the solution and shares with them a little personal insight, you can begin to think about where to place your message so it will have the best chance of reaching your prospective client. That's media.

Chapter Summary

Creating marketing pieces that speak to your ideal client isn't as hard as it might sound. I've included below a tool that I use for every marketing piece I create. These are Dan Kennedy's *Top 10 Rules for Marketing*:

Rule #1.   There will always be an offer or offer(s).

Rule #2.   There will be a reason to respond right now.

Rule #3.   You will give clear instructions.

Rule #4.   There will be tracking, measurement and accountability.

Rule #5.   Whatever brand building occurs will be a happy by-product, never bought.

Rule #6.   There will be sequential follow up.

Rule #7.   There will be strong sales copy, never vague hyperbole.

Rule #8.   In general, it should look like "mail-order advertising."

Rule #9.   Results rule. Period.

Rule #10. You will be a tough minded disciplinarian and keep your business on a strict marketing diet.

Marketing Mindset

Chapter Three:
Select the Right Media

Media is simply the vehicle for the delivery of your message, and choices are as far reaching as you can imagine. While I'm not going to create an all-inclusive list, here are a few categories just to get you thinking about all the potential outlets for your message:

Direct Mail

Post cards

ValPak

Catalog

Sales Letter

Invitation

Flyers

Publications

Yellow Pages

Magazines

Trade Journals

Press Releases

Books

Events

Trade Shows
Conventions
Workshops
Seminars

Online

Website
Facebook
Google+
Blogs
Email

Outdoor

Billboards
Vehicle Wraps
Bus Benches
Uniforms
Body Paint

Broadcast

Network Television
Subscription Video
Traditional Radio
Satellite Radio

Did this list fuel your imagination? There are so many different options for delivering your marketing message. Which is best? Which is worst? Sorry, there aren't simple answers to those questions. In fact, with respect to message delivery, there is no such thing as bad media. That doesn't mean, however, that all media is good for your business or even right for it.

One big mistake I see business owners consistently make is delegating their marketing to the next media sales representative who walks through their door. Now, generally speaking, I harbor no ill will toward media sales people. However, you must know that their motivation is to sell media. If they're any good, they're going to make a very compelling case for their media as the vehicle you need.

By way of analogy, let me give you an example of what I mean. Let's say you are in Los Angeles, and you want to deliver a detailed message to clients in New York. You have a number of options for getting your message delivered. You could post it on Facebook. You might put it into an envelope and mail it, FedEx it or hire a currier to deliver it. If you communicate often enough you might purchase a video conferencing solution. Heck, you could fly to New York and deliver it in person. There are certainly a lot of options for getting your messages where you want them to go; some cost very little money but are very inefficient, while some cost a great deal more money but may not be very efficient. Which is right?

Deciding what media will give you the most "bang for your buck" isn't the only consideration. To help you reduce the clutter and make informed media choices, Dan Kennedy offers three general rules:

1. Know your market.
2. Use as many *effective* media vehicles as possible.
3. Spend as much as you can to acquire a customer.

Let me elaborate on each of these so as to be clear.

We talked extensively earlier in the book about your target market also known as your IDEAL customer. Your choices of media will depend upon how you define your market by knowing as much as you can about them, such as geographic, demographic and psychographic information:

Geographic

- *Where do they live?*
  - o Country

- o State or Province
- o City
- o Neighborhood
- o Zip Code
- o Carrier Route

- *What do they live in?*
  - o Single Family Home
  - o Condominium
  - o Apartment
  - o Gated Community
  - o Retirement Village

Demographic

- *Who are they?*
  - o Gender
  - o Age
  - o Race
  - o Religion
  - o Income
  - o Education
  - o Nationality
  - o Disability
  - o Single
  - o Married
  - o Cohabitating
  - o No Children
  - o Young Family
  - o Empty Nester

Psychographic

- *What are their interests?*
  - o Affiliations:
  - o Professional
  - o Political
  - o Religious
  - o Recreation:
  - o Arts
  - o Music
  - o Theatre
  - o Boating
  - o Biking
  - o Travel

The more you know about your IDEAL customer, the better success you'll have in choosing media that will best reach your market and be both effective and efficient in delivering your message. But your success will also be determined by HOW you use the media, which is Dan's second point.

A flyer placed on the windshields of automobiles parked in the grocery parking lot for a buy-one-get-one sandwich at the Burger Hut located in the same shopping center may be effective at getting people to bite on your offer (literally!). Yet, a flyer placed on those same windshields offering a seat in a financial advisor's workshop on retirement planning isn't going to have the desired result. It's not that the media is bad; it's just not a good use of it.

A well-known investment company has been using a messaging strategy for years that works incredibly well at identifying new prospective clients. It begins by saying "Congratulations. If you have $500,000 or more in investments you're among the wealthiest 7% of Americans." It goes on to offer a free guide about how to avoid investment mistakes. This same message has been delivered via direct mail, television, radio and magazine, but they don't advertise in just any media. They know their ideal client in detail way beyond their prospects' $500K or more in investable assets. They know where they live, the magazines they subscribe to, the television programs they watch and the radio programs they listen to. There's nothing random about how they use these media. Their target is clear, and the media chosen is focused like a laser.

Your challenge is to try to find as many different media as possible in which to place your message. Relying upon one or just a couple of media vehicles for the delivery of your message is not only dangerous, but it's downright lazy. It has been my experience that many business owners become dependent on one, two, maybe three means of getting customers, leaving themselves very vulnerable to competition and disruption. Of course, taking on media simply to have multiple message delivery options is meaningless if the vehicles aren't effective.

It's also possible that one media working alone won't be nearly as effective as joining two or more together. For instance, one of my clients, Kathy, uses trade shows for acquiring new customers. While you may not think of trade shows as media, they can be an effective vehicle for delivering your message to a targeted audience. Kathy is in the medical technology business and each year participates in her industry's biggest trade show event, which attracts doctors, practitioners and healthcare providers from all over the world. Kathy's ideal customer is in this community. When we first met, she was relatively successful at meeting prospects at the show and creating a list of good candidates for her technology product. Kathy made an excellent living, but she worked incredibly hard throughout the year following up with her list.

Not every prospect, however, is ready to buy. In fact, at any given moment only about three percent of your ideal customers are, what I would call, rabid prospects. In other words, they have a definite problem, they know that have this problem and they are actively seeking a solution. These are buyers. However, that means ninety-seven percent of your ideal potential clients are NOT looking for your product, program or service.

If you're like Kathy, you put these ninety-seven percent in your file and follow up with them periodically. Hopefully, you happen to call them when they percolate up to the top three percent and become buyers. That leaves an awful lot to chance, not to mention a lot of tracking and scheduling of follow-up "touches."

To reduce Kathy's workload and increase the odds she would be considered the top choice when a prospect became a buyer, we created a multi-media strategy using automated systems that included direct mail, email, a newsletter, video and websites that touched that ninety-seven percent. By implementing a "Drip Marketing" media strategy, her name and products stayed in front of prospects. Her message was sure to be noticed because of the variety of media we used. The results from this automated solution included a conversion rate that skyrocketed allowing her to triple her income in the first year of implementation. THAT is an effective use of media!

The more media options you can employ that reach your prospective customer where they are, the more successfully you'll grow your business and reach your goals.

There is, however, one more piece to this puzzle that we haven't talked about yet; tracking and measurement. This hits at the heart of Dan Kennedy's third point about spending as much money as you can to get in front of your prospects. If you don't know what works, you could be throwing good money away pursuing ineffective media tactics. You can't manage what you don't measure, and in business, there's no award for participation. The marketplace does keep score and the stats help to guide us to the wins. We'll cover this in detail in the next chapter.

Chapter Summary

There are hundreds, if not thousands, of media choices that you have for reaching your IDEAL clients.

Knowing all can about your IDEAL client is the best way for choosing the media most likely to reach them.

Never choose media based upon price alone, or worse, because everyone else is doing it; they're most likely getting it wrong.

Tracking and measurement is the only means you have for holding your media accountable. Results rule. Period.

Join media together in a sequential follow up system so that your message reaches you IDEAL clients in multiple ways. Even if they're not ready to buy today you'll have erected a virtual fence around them, predisposing them to doing business with you when they are ready.

Marketing Mindset

Chapter Four:
Measure and Manage for Success

You may think the subject here is obvious! But far too many businesses, big and small, are destroyed each year because they lose sight of this basic premise.

While it's my assertion that the number one failure in nearly every business is lack of focus on an IDEAL customer, it's also quite likely that the number two reason for business failure is a lack of understanding about the numbers.

In their book, *How to Sell at Margins Higher than Your Competitors,* leading authorities on price-preservation in B2B (Business to Business) selling, Larry Steinmetz and the late Bill Brooks, assert that "most businesses that go broke do so during a period of rising sales volume." This statement shocks many people because everyone believes that businesses fail due to a lack of sales. However, business is not a game of volume; business is always a game of margin. If a business doesn't maintain gross margin at an adequate level, it's going to go broke regardless of sales volume.

Bad economics is what often happens when a business owner attempts to create a great service and a "wow" customer experience but sabotages his efforts by doing it while competing with the low price leader in his industry. A continuous flow of money is necessary to acquire customers and create a "wow" experience that has them coming back with their friends, family and other referrals.

Unfortunately, many clients come to me in their darkest hour. Remember Marty's story from earlier? He, like so many others, arrived at my door, hat-in-hand, looking for a quick fix. Because they've spent years operating on bare bones pricing, there's no money left for aggressive marketing and promotion. I'm usually met with, "I can't afford that," when I suggest creating targeted advertising, crafting and mailing an effective sales letter, providing more training for staff or even my fees for healing their sickly businesses. There is no quick fix to be had here. If you have a sound core business, though, the capital reserves and the willingness to follow my care plan for twelve to eighteen months, I can certainly help you get your business back on solid footing.

I don't say any of that here to be braggadocios or to suggest that those are the kinds of clients I'm seeking. Frankly, it's a lot of work turning a business around. I'd much rather work with business owners who prefer a proactive approach to growing their business; those who seek my involvement early on so that they can grow profitably. With all the misinformation and misunderstanding about business marketing circulating today, my clients often fall in the former category. While turnarounds are challenging and time-consuming, it is gratifying to see a business owner reconnect with the possibilities their business could offer and move from the failing column to the win.

The remainder of this chapter gets into what most business owners consider drudgery – the tracking and measuring of business success. The list provided isn't all-inclusive but does review some of the significant numbers, including some your accountant has probably never thought about.

WARNING. Paying attention to numbers is a dull, tiresome routine. The more you want to know about your business, the more numbers there will be. They cannot be skimmed. They must be read, understood, thought about and compared with other sets of numbers that you have read that day, that week or earlier that year.

Marketing Mindset

Average Transactional Value

Let's begin with average first transactional value. It gives you a big picture number from which you may be willing to spend all, some portion, or even 150 percent and more to acquire a customer. This is the starting point, a must have number for determining the maximum cost allowable for the acquisition of a new customer before spending the first dollar on advertising and marketing. Going forward, continuing to measure ATV will give you a snapshot for how well or poorly your selection of customers, sales process and salespersons are doing against benchmarks from a prior period and during special promotions.

Increasing your ATV is also one the few ways a business running at capacity can increase profitability. Small incremental increases to ATV equate to significant net profits. For example, let's assume that your current ATV equals $500.00 and that fifty percent is cost of goods sold and overhead costs consume another thirty percent; leaving you a net of $100.00 or twenty percent. If you can increase ATV by $50.00 or ten percent, and that cost of goods remains constant, then you've increased profitability by twenty-five percent. The question we must continue to ask is, "What can we do to increase ATV?"

Chapter Four: Measure and Manage for Success

Customer Value

This number takes into consideration the number of transactions and buying behavior over some period. The period will vary depending upon the business. For some, it will be a monthly or quarterly measurement, for others an annual measurement will be sufficient.

Measuring average customer value over time provides a means by which to segment customers into A's, B's and C's so that you can market to each accordingly. This also allows you to choose better media, methods and sources of customers and to understand clearly where your "A" customers are coming from versus your "C" customers. With this data firmly in hand, you can then add resources to attract the "A" customers and reduce resources that produce the "C" customers. This information can be useful in other ways, too, such as identifying salespeople who bring in "A" clients versus those who mostly bring in "C" clients. Leveraging key sales data in this way gives you the opportunity to refine sales training and hiring practices.

Contribution to Profit

CTP allows us to look deeper into what customers buy and how they behave. Most businesses, whether wholesale, retail or service providers, offer a variety

51

of goods and services at varying price and profitability, naturally making some customers more valuable than others. Additionally, even the customers who purchase the same goods and services will require differing levels of care.

By monitoring CTP, companies can determine if certain customers require so much support as to make them too costly to keep. Imagine discovering that your average customer required two to three hours of technical support annually, but that ten percent of your customers required twenty to thirty hours of technical support annually. With that powerful information, you could proactively work to get rid of the tech support heavy clients and positively impact your bottom line. If you're not measuring CTP, you are undoubtedly servicing customers who are too costly to keep.

Lifetime Customer Value

To arrive at this number, you need to employ a simple formula:

$$CV + CTP + \text{Average length of Customer retention}$$
$$= (LCV) \text{ Lifetime Customer Value}$$

The Lifetime Customer Value number will help you decide how much to invest in acquiring new customers. It's also the amount you'll use to calculate the cumulative value of your business the day you acquire a new customer or reactivate a lost one. Understanding this number will help you see the real costs of losing customers and the value of investing resources to keep them versus replacing them.

Additionally, when the time comes to sell your business, knowing this number helps to establish the business' true value beyond annual revenue or profit. And, although we're not going to get into a discussion about exit strategy in this book, creating your exit strategy with goals around your LCV will help you to determine the most opportune time to exit your business for the greatest gain.

Cost Per Lead

This is the dollars spent to get a prospect into your sales funnel or start down the sales path that you've constructed. For example, you're paying $1,000 per month to advertise in the local paper, which results in an average of ten people calling each month. Your CPL from that media is $100. CPL can often be improved significantly through the message conveyed in your marketing. Be careful not to judge too quickly here, sometimes the media with the highest CPL can provide the lowest Cost per Sale.

Cost Per Sale

This is the most critical number you'll calculate because it reflects all costs required to put a prospect into the funnel, move him through the funnel and, ultimately, convert him to a customer.

Sales Effectiveness

This isn't a specific number so much as a collection of numbers that can help you improve CPS, if analyzed correctly. Examples:

The numbers of visitors to a website who provide full contact information and invite you to follow up.

The number of people who call and are converted to kept appointments.

The numbers reflected as a closing percentage as when prospects come into your place of business or your salesperson is invited into a prospect's home/business and a presentation is made.

The number of customers who make a purchase calculated as a percentage of the total number of retail store visitors.

These are but a small example of the various interactions with prospects that need to be captured and analyzed. Tolerating poor performance in any of these areas needlessly backs up through your entire system making your CPS and CPL far too costly. Improving SE performance for closing percentage and transaction value provides competitive advantages and profitability thereby creating additional resources for even better marketing.

I suggest your goal should be to get to the point where you can afford to spend more dollars than your competition to acquire and retain customers. When you achieve that goal, you become an unstoppable force in the marketplace. However, if you find yourself on the opposite path, one of discounting to gain customers,

Marketing Mindset

recognize that if you pay attention to these numbers you can transition to a path of escalating prosperity in your business.

Chapter Summary

The numbers that your accountant assembles for you in Balance Sheets, Profit & Loss Statements, and Cash Flow Analysis are, in effect, a historical record of your business. They only tell you where you've been and don't contain the detail needed to chart improvement.

While the new numbers I've suggested here are also historical in nature, they are numbers that you use to track the effectiveness of your marketing and sales efforts.

Embrace the complexity! Your competition won't take the time because they're too busy looking for the easy button. Every truly successful business owner I know studies and understands their numbers.

Marketing Mindset

Section II:
Positioning:
Your Platform is Your
Greatest Asset

Ready, Aim, Influence!

In this next section, I'm going to delve into much of what I've learned from another great mentor of mine, Mike Koenigs. Mike is an entrepreneur, consultant, filmmaker, speaker, author and holds patents in marketing technology. He's worked with a number of celebrity clients including Paula Abdul, Tony Robbins, Tim Ferris, Dan Kennedy and Harvey Mackay.

Mike often says that if you lost all of your worldly possessions tomorrow, you'd still have your platform. That's the one thing no one can take from you. Platform is the single most important component of your life and business that you should always be building upon to accelerate your success. Your platform consists of who knows you, your area of expertise (knowledge), prospect/client list, reach, speaking topics, products, services, media contacts and connections.

The greater your platform, the easier it becomes to rise from the ashes if things do crash around you. So even if you don't have a big platform now, stay tuned. The information shared in the next couple of chapters combined with the concepts we learned in the first section of this book will give you the tools to elevate your platform.

Chapter Five:
Position Yourself as Expert

There's a revolution taking place in the world today. Have you noticed? While millions are suffering through a tough economy, millions more are helping to shape an entirely new economy. You might want to pay attention here, because everything you thought you knew about work and employment is changing. It's changing the way people see employment and it's changing the way small businesses operate. Don't skip over this section of the book or you'll miss it.

So just what is this change? It goes by a number of names but I call it "Expert Positioning." I've even created an entire program called Expert Position Marketing™ to help my clients take advantage of this new world order. In his book, "The Charge," Brendon Burchard calls it "entrepreneurial expertise." Whatever you call it, the result is the same. Millions of business people and small solopreneur business owners are moving away from the idea of "knowledge worker" and toward packaging their knowledge and wisdom to position themselves as experts.

You can see this change all around you. Perhaps you didn't realize that it was an entirely new economy. You can see it most clearly when someone starts producing articles, podcasts, videos, online training and books that others can buy. You see experts popping up all around, if you look. If you haven't noticed this trend, I urge to you pay close attention because if you don't figure out how to emulate these folks and become the expert in your niche, you may find yourself irrelevant. After all, no one seeks the guru at the bottom of the mountain.

You might be thinking, "I'm no expert." I'd like to encourage you to think about it this way. At some point, you didn't know all you know now about the technical aspects of your business, some piece of equipment, or a process for efficiently completing some task. Perhaps you've become pretty proficient in a hobby, athletic endeavor or recreational activity. It may have taken years of learning to perfect your skills. You may have even picked up a few tricks, shortcuts or secrets along the way. My point is there are others, perhaps millions of others, who would love to know what you know. To these folks, you're an expert!

Building your platform starts with the power of positioning. You have to establish yourself as the go-to authority in your niche. When positioned properly, you instantly increase your value. You can charge two times, five times, maybe even ten times more money for sharing your expertise. The media will seek you out, and you can leverage your authority and credibility to build your business. As your platform elevates, you become incomparable, both competition and recession proof. You become irresistibly attractive to prospects, customers and the media.

There are three key strategies for positioning yourself as the expert:

1. Create your story
2. Create Positioning Content
3. Build Your Presence Online and Offline

Create Your Story. The ultimate purpose for creating your story is to help your audience develop a bond with you through understanding what it is you stand for. Remember the furniture store I referenced earlier that talks about spaying and neutering your pets? That's an example of what they stand for. Even if you're in a crowded niche surrounded by thousands of other experts, your unique story allows people to get to know you. When they can relate to you, they'll like and trust you. Differentiating yourself creates the emotional connection that separates you from your competition. For those who resonate and relate to your story, you will stand out like a beacon in the night.

That's why it's important to be aware of the elements of your story that are like those of your audience. Identifying the elements that help them identify more closely with you will gently push your audience's bond with you. They will see you as "one of them." Add in aspects that build trust between you and your audience, and you will gain followers eager to learn from you. Trust is probably the most important piece of this puzzle. Prospects can know you, they can like you but if they don't trust you, they will not work with you. Creating trust is crucial.

Create Positioning Content. Positioning content consists of the components you want your audience to find when they search for you online. As you are creating your biography, articles, video, and other content be sure to include keywords that relate to your topic, and not your talent. This helps with search engine rankings, and makes it easier for those searching to know that your content is what they were looking for.

Your USP, or Unique Selling Proposition, is a short statement that differentiates you from everyone else in your field. You don't want to sound like everyone else in your field. If someone asked you "What do you do?"

and you were unable to say something that no one else in your area of expertise would say your USP has failed. You must be able to articulate the unique value you bring to the table. Otherwise, you become a commodity.

Remember the Domino's Pizza's USP?

> *Fresh hot pizza delivered to your door*
> *within 30 minutes ... Guaranteed*

Your USP will take some work, and it should answer your prospect's question, "Why should I choose to do business with you versus any and every other option available?"

One easy formula to use is: I do X to Y even if Z.

For example: "I teach dentists to do social media marketing even if they've never turned on a computer before." Your USP is a succinct sentence that clearly describes what you do and for whom you do it. Stating your USP succinctly has another benefit. It makes it easy for others to tell the world about you, too. "My friend Mark teaches dentists to do social media marketing even if they've never turned on a computer before." As soon as someone else can articulate your expertise this clearly, your footprint is established.

Build your Presence. Positioning is all of your content, accomplishments and internet presence coming together to form a clear picture of you in the minds of your audience. The unique elements that you weave throughout these components differentiate you from everyone else in your niche and establish you as the expert.

In addition to what you create online, whether it is on your blog site, a website or social media, you want to look for opportunities to speak to audiences of qualified prospects. This could be live on stage or in a webinar/teleseminar format but it's important to seek out these opportunities. Your local chambers of commerce, fraternal organizations and community event planners are always looking for speakers to fill their events.

Another way to be seen as the expert is to provide articles and content of relevance to the local news media. This is not the place to promote your business, but it is a great place to offer topical information regarding your expertise as it relates to current events. News reporters are always looking for sources for their stories and interviews every day. In fact, there are over 10,000 radio interviews conducted each day. Why aren't they interviewing you?

Think about the folks you see interviewed regularly on various news programs often referred to as the "expert" for the topic of the day. In most cases, these people first presented themselves as experts by offering relevant information to the reporters and noting their contact information for follow up questions. Being the featured go-to expert on your topic changes the way you're perceived in the marketplace, and it's not that hard to get local media attention. You could be writing a monthly article for one of your industry trade publications allowing you to reach your target audience directly. Imagine your main business is providing services to automobile dealers and you have a column each month in "Dealer Magazine." Who reads this magazine? You can bet your target market of owners of automobile dealerships do!

Chapter Summary

Your platform consists of who knows you, your area of expertise (knowledge), prospect/client list, reach, speaking topics, products, services, media contacts and connections.

There are, perhaps, millions of people who would love to know what you know. To these folks, you're an expert.

Create your story. Build some of your own personal story into your marketing, allow your clients get to know the real you.

Create positioning content so when potential prospects search for you or the solution to their problems, they find you "out there" as the expert.

Build your expert presence through speaking, writing and providing relevant content to reporters. You might want to check out www.helpareporter.com as a resource.

Chapter Six:
Get Published

I saved this topic for its own chapter, because publishing your book is THE best way I know to open doors and build your presence. If you can lead your pitch to the local news media, or community event planner with "Hi, I'm John Doe, number one bestselling author of "Your Book," you get their immediate attention.

Think about this for a moment. There are over seven billion people worldwide, over 300 million live here in the United States, but there are only about three million authors. When you become a published author, you are part of a select group; as a bestselling author, you're in an even more elite group. How's that for differentiation?

Being an author instantly makes you an expert. People's perceptions change. You're no longer a "me-too" business; you're the one who wrote the book. Your credibility among clients and competitors soars as an author. (Your competitors might be a wee bit jealous, too.) You're no longer like the rest, they haven't published a book. If, instead of handing your prospect your business card just like everyone else, you slide a copy of your book across the table. Suddenly, you're seen differently, you're seen as the expert. They'll sit up and take notice. They may have originally taken the meeting as a favor or nice gesture, but as soon as you hand them your book, you become a welcome guest. They're now predisposed to doing business with you.

Consumers have a multitude of choices today. Do you want to talk about something other than price? By being unique, it will position you to exceed your clients' expectations. Being an author demonstrates you've gone the extra mile. Being an author will tip the scales in your favor time and time again.

So how does one go about writing such a book? Well there are probably as many answers to that question as there are people, but as you'll see, the process is very similar to many of the things we've already talked about in this book.

Surveys have found that hundreds of millions of people say they want to write a book, yet only a small percentage ever actually does. Usually it's because people don't know how to begin. They become paralyzed in uncertainty until their initial desire turns to fear, overwhelm, stress or all of the above.

Bestselling author, Brian Tracy, has written over fifty-five books and been published in over fifty countries. His goal is to write five books every year. To date, he has written more than one book per year on average for the past twenty years, most in as little as ninety days. At this pace, he may well be one of the most prolific writers of all time.

What's his secret?

Tracy explains that ninety percent of any project is consumed in the effort it takes to get started. In the words of Confucius, "A journey of a thousand miles begins with a single step."

Don't wait until you have all the information, resources, time, data, energy, facts, money, education or any number of other things to get going. Simply start. Your only needed resource is a burning desire. In fact, there are only four simple steps to success in any endeavor:

1. Embrace a tremendous desire.
2. Try it.
3. Get Feedback.
4. Repeat until you succeed.

Once you set the process in motion, it will take care of itself. First, you must press, "GO."

Think of a topic you really care about that will appeal to your ideal client. Choosing a topic that grips you is imperative. Start with a subject you know well and have immersed yourself in. You need to have an enormous amount of mental capital on your subject matter before you can begin writing on it.

I've learned from Mike Koenigs that one of the fastest and easiest ways to create a book is to use the top ten most frequently asked questions about your products or services you hear repeatedly in your business. As you write each question, provide the answer, too.

Next, consider the questions you wish they would ask or should be asking. These are the important points that will differentiate you from your competitors. Write the questions and answers from this new list. Between these sets of questions and answers, you're starting to compile a tidy bit of information.

Another system I use to begin writing is called "down dumping" or "mind dump." This process is simple – get the details out of your head and onto paper by letting your ideas flow without hesitation, judgment or analytic thought. Write until you can write no more. Then I suggest you walk away from this for a day or two. When you come back and review your free-flowing thoughts, you may identify some areas you need to expand upon or have forgotten to include. Once you feel you have all the pertinent information in the dump, you can move to the next step.

As you peruse your "data dump," start to think in terms of chapters and organization. Try to put yourself in the shoes of your ideal client. How would he or she want to see the information structured? Consider what the logical flow would be for someone who knows nothing about your topic. Remember, you are the expert and it's easy to forget that you know far more than your audience does. When you feel you have a handle on the flow, write your table of contents.

Congratulations! You've just overcome the biggest hurdle to writing a book – getting started and having a plan!

You're not done yet, though. The information you have currently could be a bit thin in the substance arena so you'll want to beef up each chapter with related subtopics. It's not time to analyze here, just continue writing down everything that comes to you. As you progress, you'll start to see the linkage between chapters and ideas, and connections for how the information can flow. You'll probably be astonished at the shear mass of content you've created.

I again recommend you set this aside for a day or so to allow your brain to rest. It's vitally important that you come back to this work with fresh eyes and a clear head to make certain you haven't left out something important. Keep in mind, you're not giving away all your trade secrets but sharing helpful information your audience could use. You want to give them a taste of what working with you can be like, not put your entire business in a book.

It's likely your book is now a loosely constructed set of sentences, unfinished thoughts and sentence fragments. This is the time to analyze your information and create true structure within each chapter. How you do this is up to your personal preference. I prefer to dictate to create a conversational tone to my writing. I also believe dictating imparts my enthusiasm for my subject better than if I type it. Someone else may feel more comfortable at a keyboard typing his or her thoughts. There is no right or wrong way to do this, but it is a necessary step to bring a cohesive and logical flow into your book. How long this takes is totally up to you. The good news is you don't have to follow a linear process to write your book. If you are "supposed" to be writing chapter three one day, but you really feel like working on chapter five, then work on chapter five. You can always weave in transitions and chapter-to-chapter continuity later.

You can write your introduction at any point in the process. You'll want to welcome the reader and reveal some special offer. The purpose for the introduction is to bring people deeper into what it is that you do, and to give them an opportunity to get to know you by sharing some personal information. Then make an offer for some bonus information, videos, or perhaps a webinar that allows them to engage with you further.

The final chapter of your book is a review of the material with an emphasis on next steps. Keep in mind that anyone who has read your entire book and gotten to this chapter is likely ready for more. Don't disappoint them. Don't just give them next steps, however. Provide opportunities in which they can engage with you or get more content from you.

Whew! When you get to this point, you might think you're done. This is, to use writer's parlance, your "first draft." Know that you are the expert on your information, so you must be the one to read and reread your manuscript until you believe it is as good as it can be. Don't go crazy with this, however. Perfection isn't the goal, but a reasonably well written and organized book is. So do yourself a favor and review, revise and rewrite as necessary. Ask friends and relatives to read it and give feedback – understanding these same people can be either too nice or too harsh. Always take comments with a grain of salt. Only after you have done your own editing is your book ready for the next step...more editing.

You might be groaning, but hiring a professional editor to work through your book is a necessary expense. Our brains have a limited capacity for reading the same things repeatedly. At some point, we stop seeing grammatical or typographical errors because our brain "fixes" them. In addition, we may not see where information could be missing or misplaced in the document. You can bet a professional editor will see all these things and much more. He or she will test links you've added and other resources, too. It's simply critical that a fresh pair of eyes edit your content. A great editor will take your work and polish it into a book that reads well and one you are truly proud to put your name on.

After all of this work is complete, you are ready to publish. Hopefully, you will not have waited until this moment to investigate the variety of publishing options available today. Do you only want an online presence? Then Kindle might be a good option. Do you want a hard or paperback copy to give away in person or use as your "big business card?" Then you'll want to research the dozens of self-publishing companies and the options they provide before making a decision. It never hurts to ask others who have published a book what company they used, what their experience was like and if they would use that company again. Also, look at the bookplates of books you think are formatted well to find the publisher information.

If you're hoping a "named" publisher, such as Random House, Rodale Press, University Press, etc., will pick up your book, be prepared to be rejected unless you already have other books published that have sold well. It is difficult today to get the attention of big publishing houses. They work on thin margins, so they are less inclined to take chances on unknown authors unless the manuscript is outstanding and tackles a topic in a new and different way. It isn't impossible to be picked up by a big publisher, but it takes time, extra effort and a thick skin. In addition, they often take a huge chunk of book sale profits and do little to no marketing for their authors. I was less concerned about having a known publisher; I simply wanted to get my book into the hands of the people who needed it most – my prospects – in the quickest and most convenient format possible.

Marketing Mindset

Ultimately, it's your decision on where you publish your book. Just begin the hunt early in your book writing adventure versus waiting until the book is finished.

Chapter Summary

Writing a book is a great way to differentiate you and your business in the marketplace. It's never been easier to get your book published these days, especially given that Amazon has effectively done to the book publishing business what Apple did to the music industry.

Mike Koenigs uses a number of strategies for writing his books such as interviewing other experts and teaching various marketing strategies in webinars. He has the information collected or presented transcribed and edited into book form. One of the easiest methods Mike teaches for getting started is his 10x10 formula:

Write down the top ten frequently asked questions customers ask about your product or service.

Write down the top ten questions a potential buyer SHOULD be asking about your product or service. These are the important things that differentiate you from your competitors that you WISH they would ask you.

Record a one to three-minute video response to each question.

Have the whole thing transcribed and edited into book form.

If you want to see an example of this formula, you can check out a book that Mike Koenigs created called *"Podcast Strategies / How to Podcast – 21 Questions Answered."* You can also check out Mike Koenigs latest book *"Publish and Profit"* on Amazon for more in depth strategies and guidance on this topic.

Chapter Seven:
Promote and Profit

Your book's been published; it's listed on Amazon…. now what? Now the real work begins. But don't fret, this is the fun work! This is where you get to share your passion with the world. You may have heard about various authors being paid an advance to write their next book. What they're really being paid to do is to promote their next book. That's why you hear them being interviewed on the radio, on television and in newspapers and magazines flying around the country for weeks or months doing six to eight interviews each day. In a sense, that's what you're going to do to. Maybe not in the national press, probably not all over the country, but you do have to promote yourself.

Start by leveraging your book to get meetings with potential clients, speaking gigs at association meetings where potential clients gather, trade show presentations or events hosted by other experts in your field. It won't be hard. Here is how I introduce myself when calling possible prospects, "Hi, my name is Mark Klipsch, number one bestselling author of "*Marketing Mindset: The Ultimate Guide to Positioning Yourself as the Go-*

To Expert in Your Niche. " As part of my book release, I'm doing a speaking tour where I teach small business owners to increase sales exponentially using the power of expert positioning. Would you like for me to speak at your association meeting?"

You'll find you're often well received with this kind of introduction. Event producers are always looking for speakers and will feel confident about booking someone who has a bestselling book on a topic relevant to their audience.

When you stand on stage and begin speaking about your topic, there's instant credibility. Wait, I know what you're thinking, "public speaking, oh hell no...that's not me." While public speaking is certainly among people's greatest fears, please realize two things: one, sometimes the worse you are at public speaking, the more human you appear to your audience, and two, when you speak from the heart on a subject that you're passionate about, that passion comes through to your audience. If you're too polished, it comes off as cold and less authentic. Also, realize that everybody feels nervous. I've heard it said that Johnny Carson, who hosted "The Tonight Show" nearly every night for 30 years, vomited before going on stage each night.

The real point here is that you'll get clients from speaking opportunities. Depending upon where you get booked to speak, you may be permitted to make a direct pitch for your products or services from the stage. But even if not, don't be discouraged. Often just articulating a problem and making it clear that you have a solution to that problem by seeding your products and services into your talk will have potential clients seeking you out afterward. Offering to send them a free copy of your book in exchange for them paying the shipping costs is a great way to get your book in their hands and get you their contact information.

Promoting is only one-half of the equation. The other is profit. My grandfather used to say "Son, it's all for naught until you ring the cash register!" I'll conclude this chapter with three keys to profitability regardless of your business.

First, no one seeks the guru at the bottom of the mountain. STOP GIVING AWAY YOUR KNOWLEDGE FOR FREE. One of the most powerful things you can do to position yourself as the expert, as the guru at the top of the mountain, is to understand fully the value of your knowledge. There's an old adage that says, "In the land of the blind, the one-eyed man is king." You need to understand the value of the solutions you provide to your customers and understand that not all customers will value the solutions equally. Frequently, the solution you provide will have a much greater impact for one client versus another. By selling the solution at a price you deem commensurate for the time it takes you to perform, you run the risk that the client who receives a lesser benefit perceives your price too high, and, conversely, the client who stands to reap great benefit perceives your price to low thereby discrediting you as the right solution.

The better question to ask is, "What's the value of my solution to THIS customer?" You can calculate this value in terms of increased transactions, increased revenue per sale, decreased cost per month, and so on. The important thing to understand is the benefit to your customer so that you can speak about your solution in those terms and offer it at a price commensurate with the value or benefit your client will receive by implementing that solution. The key here is to put yourself in the position of your client and imagine how much their business or life will change with the products and services you provide.

The next thing you have to do is to project confidence. Whether on stage in front of an audience or in the office of a potential client, people will sense your certainty and that conviction will help you close them. How would you react to a doctor or consultant who appeared timid or nervous? Do you want them doing surgery or working for you in any capacity? Me either!

Confidence comes from knowing that you have a solution that works, but also not being committed to a particular outcome. Gather testimonials and other social proof from clients that you've already helped and display it in all of your positioning collateral online and offline. Potential clients will be influenced by what others have to say about you, but more importantly, it will help you to project confidence in your presentation. It's important that you realize you're not going to close every sale or win every opportunity. If you can enter a conversation, whether on stage or one-on-one and be okay with the client saying no (even if you know that you're not going to eat tonight if you don't make this sale), you'll win more often because the audience won't sense your desperation.

The third and final key to your perception as the guru at the top of the mountain is to make yourself strategically unavailable. To follow up on my last comment about not being perceived as desperate, don't set your own appointments, answer your own calls, or do anything that makes it appear you're not busy with other clients. For example, if a client or potential client sends you an email or leaves a voice message, don't reply right away. Unless it's truly a matter of life or death (and it never is), don't be afraid to make your clients wait to reach you or schedule an appointment to talk with you. As the expert, you can't be readily available; people come to you, not the other way around.

Chapter Summary

Become a shameless self-promoter; if you won't blow your own horn, who will? Get comfortable promoting yourself and looking for opportunities to be interviewed and to speak to groups about your topic.

In the land of the blind, the one-eyed man is king. If you don't value your information and expertise, no one else will either.

Understand the value of your solution to your client and price accordingly whenever possible.

Project confidence and conviction in everything you do. If you believe in yourself and your solution, others will too.

Limit your accessibility. Nothing screams desperation more than being available 24/7 to anyone and everyone who calls, emails, or texts. Block time in your day to return calls, answer emails and texts and otherwise follow up with clients and prospects.

Marketing Mindset

Section III:
Formula:
Wash, Rinse and Repeat

In this final section, I want to share some of the wisdom of Frank Kern. I believe this could be the most brilliant business development strategy ever.

Frank Kern is considered to be the highest paid and most in-demand direct response internet info-marketing consultant and copywriter on the planet. He is credited with having engineered the highest grossing information-marketing promotions in the history of the industry. Frank has also served as advisor to noted celebrities such as Tony Robbins, Neil Strauss, Dean Graziosi and more. He has also, like me, been a student of Dan Kennedy for many years.

While there are many things that set Frank Kern apart from most, I think his difference can be summed up in the one statement he often says, "If you want to influence your prospects and turn them quickly into customers, demonstrate you can help them by actually helping them."

Marketing Mindset

I know that sounds kind of simple, and maybe obvious. But who really does that?

You may be asking why I titled this section "Formula: Wash, Rinse and Repeat." Well, I've watched Frank develop this strategy and then continue to repeat it again and again to win new business and generate millions in revenue every year. I decided not to reinvent the wheel. When you find someone who's successful, study what he or she is doing, adapt it to fit your business, implement, tweak it when necessary, then WASH, RINSE, REPEAT!

In this last section, I will take you through the basics of the strategy that Frank teaches to his client base of coaches and consultants. Then I'll give some examples for how this strategy can be applied to a variety of other businesses. I want to emphasize here and encourage you to look outside your particular industry to see what others are doing and think about how you might apply a similar strategy in your own business. Show up differently, stand apart from the crowd, don't be ordinary and you'll be amazed at the results you can achieve.

Chapter Eight:
Build a Powerful, Repeatable Method

You're lucky, your competitors have a disposable mentality when it comes to prospects and customers. This is a belief that if the customer doesn't buy now, they'll never get another shot to buy at the current price/ rate/etc. Their presentations are therefore, salesy, sleazy even; with lots of scarcity wrapped around huge claims and nothing but sales pressure. They beat customers into submission with an attitude of "buy or die." You've probably experienced this firsthand at some point in your life.

These sales tactics suck for the customer, but you can use your competitor's bad behavior to your advantage. Your customers and prospects are searching, in an almost desperate fashion, for businesses that will actually treat them with dignity and respect. Do this, treat them with dignity and respect and they'll love you. Make them feel special and they'll reward you with their continued business and referrals for years to come. Sounds pretty simple, doesn't it?

I want to dig a little deeper into what everyone else does to get customers. I want to be sure you fully understand what I'm saying so you don't copy what you see every day in newspapers, on billboards, on television, and in sales presentations, etc. We can't keep repeating what we've always done and seen others do, and expect we're going to get better or even different results.

So what's the first message you almost always see? It usually begins with statements about how awesome they are, how long they've been in business, a listing of their credentials and a multitude of other chest pounding fluff. Blah, blah, blah, blah, blah, right? Now, crazy thing is most marketing stops right there. Take a look around. I'd be willing to bet that if you grab your newspaper, drive down the highway and look at the billboards, thumb through the direct marketing material that shows up in your mailbox today, or listen to the next sales presentation offered, you'll see that I've just described at least eighty percent or more of all the advertisements you read and presentations you hear. Rarely will you see a call to action or hear an offer and if you do, it typically says the equivalent of "Buy my stuff now." It's absolutely horrible, the worst approach ever. But you see/hear it every day.

There's certainly nothing about this that gives you, as a potential customer, confidence that the business can actually solve your problem. If you happen to be desperately seeking a solution you might give them a call, but only because you may rationalize that if they been in business for fifty years, they must be okay or something similar. You're not calling because they have done anything in their marketing to demonstrate or create any confidence that they can ACTUALLY solve your problem, though.

So what's the secret to building that confidence? Let me walk you through what Frank calls the client-centric model. Think about how you might implement this in your marketing. You begin by not talking about yourself much, if at all. Your clients and prospects don't give a rat's ass about all the things that you do, how long you've been doing it, or how many credentials or accolades you've received! They care only about one thing. Can you solve their problem and make their life better?

Instead of talking about what you can do, demonstrate that you can help them by actually helping them. I know that sounds simple, but bear with me while I illustrate.

Just suppose you're at home participating in an important phone call when the doorbell rings unexpectedly. You ignore it, but the pest outside continues to ring. By now, the dog is barking, too. You're determined to stay on the call, so you walk into the bedroom, close the door and continue your conversation. The doorbell finally stops ringing, but just about the time you think the pest has gone away, you hear him banging on the windows. Angrily, you nearly pull the curtains off the rod as you push them aside to look out the window. That's when your mouth falls open. Your neighbor's house is on fire, and your home is about to catch fire, too. This Good Samaritan is merely trying to alert you to the danger. The annoying pest has quickly become a welcome guest.

That's exactly the situation we're going to create in our formula. I'm going to show you how, but without burning down your or your neighbors' homes.

Client Centric Model

We start by driving traffic to an online opt-in page with a compelling offer. Details to come just stay with me for a minute. We then follow up immediately with a multi-step process, which includes irresistible intrigue, and leads to the final step where the prospect qualifies him to you. Then you turn that prospect into a customer by using a collaborative closing process.

So let's break this down a little further. There are thousands of ways to generate traffic. Many business owners are drawn to online media sources because they are fairly inexpensive; however, I've had tremendous response from direct mail. It truly is a secret weapon if you know how to use it. Whichever way you choose, just as I mentioned at the start of this book, you have to understand the person or business you're looking to attract. Nearly all media has demographic information about their audience, so if you're looking for financial professionals, they know how to reach them. Remember, the more you know about your target audience, the easier it is to locate them. Because, as a society, we have revealed so much information about ourselves both online and through participation in customer loyalty programs, you have never had such an incredible opportunity to get in front of your perfect audience more quickly and easily than you do today.

Now that you know whom they are and where to find them, you need to generate leads. To do that, find out the most logical question your prospects are asking themselves and then tailor your offer to answer their question for *free*.

Let's use an example from residential real estate. Most everyone has bought, sold or lived in a home, so this should be familiar. A local real estate broker wants to generate leads from people living in an exclusive neighborhood in her town. She wants the homeowners to choose her to list their home when they are ready to sell. One way to generate leads is by using a free report. The broker knows this, so she wrote a free report entitled, "The 7 Questions You Must Ask A Realtor Before You List Your Home For Sale." She made the report available to her target market. Interested homeowners requested the report and she followed up with them. She received a decent response rate and some homeowners listed their home with her because of her report. However, marketing in this way is a little more push than pull. A bigger problem is that it screams "salesperson." It won't get as good a response because the broker is attempting to get the homeowner's attention in a way that may or may not serve them.

Perhaps a better way to generate leads is to give them the most obvious thing they're looking for and continue to help them until they raise their hands and say, "Thank you so much, can you just help me out a little more?"

Let's continue using the real estate example. You are the owner of a luxury home in an exclusive neighborhood called Park Place. You've raised your children there and now you're ready to downsize. If you're like most people, your first question before listing your house is likely to be, "I wonder how much we can sell the house for?" There may be other questions, but this is a logical first question. In fact, I posit that, "Who should we list the house with?" is probably way down on the list of questions you'd be asking in the early stages of this thought process. A smart broker will capitalize on this natural first question by giving away a report to Park Place homeowners showing Park Place home sale prices for the previous twelve months. If I'm out there thinking about selling my home and wonder how much I can sell it for and I see an ad that says, "Thinking of selling your house? Here's a free report of Park Place home sale prices for the last twelve months." I'm probably going to respond to that because it's pretty compelling.

What makes this approach work better than the other one discussed above is there's no evidence of commercial intent. Second, it attracts interested people who will need a broker's help. Third, it actually helps them with no strings attached. It's not a fluff piece. The final thing it does is it sets the broker up for the next step, which is to get the homeowners to raise their hands and say, "Please help me."

Here is the sequence of steps you'll take your prospects through:

1. An Offer to Help for Free
2. Explain the Benefits of Your Help

3. Explain Why You're Doing This
4. Eliminate Sales Fear
5. Create Irresistible Intrigue
6. Takeaway Non-Selling
7. Qualify

In the first step of the seven-step sequence, you thank them for their interest and offer to help them further for free. This could be sent in the form of a video, letter or email. In it you might say, *"In the attached report, you'll notice that two nearly identical homes had dramatically different sale prices. Would you like me to show you how one got such a great price and how you can get the most money for your house too?"* That's it, Stop! That's you offering to help them further, for free.

Second, you're going to explain the benefits of your help. Here you could say something like: *"I'm happy to help you design a custom marketing plan for your home, identify your perfect target market of prospective buyers and show you how to present your home to them for the maximum price possible. This way you'll sell your house quickly and get the highest price you can without wasting time or money. There's no cost to this or obligation of any kind."* You've just explained the benefits that your help will provide. In those couple of sentences, you've spelled out the benefits, without belaboring it or going on forever about it.

The third step in the sequence is to explain why you're doing this. People are inherently skeptical; they are probably starting to wonder what the catch is for your service. You're going to tell them in the most transparent and forthcoming way. *"I offer this free service because I'm a realtor and I sell Park Place homes exclusively. There's a good possibility that I already have a buyer who might be interested in your house especially considering the recent demand for properties like yours. So if you find value in the help I give you, you might want me to sell your home for you."* And that's it. You're not telling them how great you are, just telling like it is. You're a realtor, that's why you offer to help. You're also not selling, so they'll appreciate that, as well as your honesty.

Once you lay this all out there is the risk they will say, "Oh no, a salesperson…run!" That's why, in the fourth step in our sequence, you eliminate their fear. Here's a simple sentence you could use. *"With that said, please understand that I'm not offering a sales pitch in disguise. I promise not to pressure you or pester you in any way. In fact, if you feel I've wasted your time…."* Jim Rohn used to say, enter the conversation that's already going on in the client's mind. You just promised that you weren't going to pressure or pester them, and you promised that this isn't a sales pitch in disguise. You've addressed what was going on in their mind, saying that's not what this is.

The fifth step is really important. Kern calls this irresistible intrigue. Where you left off the phrase "in *fact, if I wasted your time...,*" insert some sort of bribe. *"Let me know and I'll write you a check,"* or *"I'll give you a gift,"* or offer something that they would find of value. Whatever you choose, make it irresistible to them. By doing this, you completely alleviate their fears. They can't help but think to themselves, "This guy's offering to help me and if I think he's wasted my time he's going to give me X, and it costs me nothing." That's irresistible! But it also adds intrigue because your prospect also can't help but think, "Wow, this guy's so confident. I just have to know what he has that gives him so much confidence that he believes he can help me." When you position yourself with that much confidence, your prospect will automatically have an increased level of confidence in you as well.

Now they're intrigued, they believe you can help them and they're beginning to get interested. That's where step six comes in. This is where you begin to protect yourself by starting to take it away. This is an incredibly powerful psychological trigger. In their mind, they're thinking, "I have *nothing to lose, this is great.*" So you begin taking it all away by saying something like, *"Before we go any further, you need to know that I simply can't help everybody. In fact, I can only be of help to people whose homes are in Park Place, are in excellent condition, not in foreclosure, etc."* This is where you begin listing all the criteria they must have in order to work with you. In other words, this is where you list the criteria of your ideal client. This protects you from the time-wasters and tire kickers and demonstrates to them that you're not just another salesperson. You are showing up differently. It's unlikely they've ever run into anyone who's said, *"I cannot work with everybody. Here are the people I'm willing to work with."* You've put yourself into a position of authority and by doing so will cause them to start listing reasons why you should work with them.

That brings us to the seventh and last step in this process: qualification. Remember though, you're not qualifying them; they're going to qualify themselves *to you.* You listed your criteria, made it irresistible and built some intrigue along the way. Whether you are speaking to them in print, in an audio or video, or from the stage, the media you use to deliver the message isn't as important as the message. You'll say something like, "Here's what you need to do next. *If you want to schedule a planning session with me, (click the link below, go to this website, call this phone number, etc.), to answer some quick questions about your home and what you're looking to accomplish. Once I have the information, I'll verify that you've met the criteria, do some market research for you and have my assistant contact you to set up some time to review it together.*" When they go to the form and answer your questions, they're qualifying themselves to you. You've effectively reversed the selling process and it works! They wouldn't be asking you to help them if they weren't interested in becoming a client because you told them what to do, and they complied.

In this example, you were completely forthright in telling them, I'm a realtor, I list houses and maybe I can help you. There was no guesswork, no surprises. You gave them instructions, and they are essentially applying to speak with you by answering your questions. You are now protected from dealing with anyone who's not your ideal client because you would never talk to anyone whose answers indicated he or she wasn't a good match for you.

So there you have Frank Kern's formula for generating leads from your ideal clients. In the last chapter, we're going to talk about how to convert them into clients.

Chapter Eight: Build a Powerful, Repeatable Method

I'm going to walk you through my process and show you exactly how I get my clients. This way, you can see firsthand how I've applied everything I've discussed in this book.

Chapter Summary

Treat your clients with dignity and respect and they'll love you. Make them feel special, and they'll reward you with their continued business and referrals for years to come.

Most business owners and salespersons blather on and on about how great they are, how long they've been in business, and the accolades they've received. Instead of talking about what you can do for your clients, demonstrate that you can help them by actually helping them.

Position yourself as a welcome guest rather than an annoying pest.

What is the one question that your prospects really want answered? It's much deeper than the obvious. Identify that one question and then build a lead generation tool that offers the answer.

Don't forget to follow the seven steps in the Client Centric Model. It will set you apart from everyone else.

1. An Offer to Help for Free
2. Explain the Benefits of Your Help

3. Explain Why You're Doing This
4. Eliminate Sales Fear
5. Create Irresistible Intrigue
6. Takeaway Non-Selling
7. Qualify

Marketing Mindset

Chapter Nine:
Execute It Again and Again

As review, we started by talking about knowing who your ideal client is and, perhaps more importantly, who is NOT your ideal client. Once we determine who they are, what's important to them, where their pain is and what's driving them, we can craft messaging that speaks to them and attracts them to you. Only then, can we look at the various media options and determine the best ones to reach your prospects. Dan Kennedy has been instrumental in my education of these key principles, and I shall be forever grateful.

In section two, we talked about building your platform and promoting you as an expert in your marketplace. We discussed how to leverage your expert positioning for opportunities to speak on stage and be interviewed by the media. And, we outlined what platform means and how to positon YOU as the guru at the top of the mountain. I credit this knowledge to my mentor Mike Koenigs, without whom the concept of building and leveraging platform would still be a mystery.

Marketing Mindset

Finally, I offered you Frank Kern's formula for lead generation which when implemented demonstrates your authority in the marketplace and has your prospects begging you to take them as clients.

As promised, I'll show you how I've put this knowledge to work in my business for a program that I offer called my "Experts Alliance Mastermind."

Let me begin by telling you a little about my "why." Simon Sinek, author of the book *"Start with Why"* says "People don't buy what you do; they buy why you do it. What you do simply proves what you believe" I've always been fascinated by business. As I've gotten older, I realize that I can always make more money, but I can't make more time. There are a number of organizations and causes that I support, but because time is my most precious resource, I choose to leverage my time where I get the greatest return, helping businesses to grow, expand and create jobs. Why? Because I truly believe that most of the world's problems can be solved by helping more entrepreneurs start and thrive in businesses in my community and throughout the world.

My ideal clients are professional service providers, such as doctors, attorneys, financial services consultants and contractors. My clients typically generate revenues of $2 million to $10 million dollars annually, so they are not likely to be solopreneurs. They are investing at least $100,000 to $500,000 annually in marketing, are frustrated by the results, struggle to calculate the ROI in their marketing and have a significant number of clients who aren't ideal. They are politically and socially conservative in their ideology, and give back to their communities through involvement in a variety of activities outside their businesses. I have a great deal of geographic, demographic and psychographic information I've gathered as well, but will leave that out for the sake of brevity.

The messaging I use is a sixteen-page sales letter entitled, "The 10 Most Powerful Advertising Rules that Your Media Sales Representatives Don't Want You to Know." This letter is mailed directly to the CEO based upon the dollars the company spends on advertising. If you'd like to have a copy to see as example, I'm happy to send it to you for the $3.95 cost of postage and handling.

Visit www.MarketingMindsetBook.com/salesletter to request a copy, and I'll mail it off to you directly.

In the sales letter, my prospects go through the same process I outlined for you in the realtor example in the last chapter. I offer to show them how to significantly increase their revenue by making a few simple corrections to their current advertising, copies of which I include in the letter, and offer a gourmet dinner for two if they think I've wasted their time. And that's before they ever become a client, of course!

No one yet has requested the certificate for the gourmet dinner. But with an offer like that, I have to be on my toes. So here's how I protect myself. When a prospect requests an appointment to talk with me, he or she fills out a short online questionnaire that asks some basic questions about their business, annual revenues, current marketing initiatives, challenges they might be experiencing and sales or revenue goals for the next year or two.

I only schedule appointments after I've read their answers, had a chance to do some homework and determined that I can actually help them. Based upon the information they've submitted, I already have a pretty good idea how I'm going to advise them. I already know they meet my criteria for business size and that they have a good reputation in their marketplace. I know they're generating leads and that they have clients. Most importantly, I know they're willing to invest in their success. In other words, before I ever talk with them, I know they're a perfect match.

Remember, the people I'm talking to are people who have specifically asked for my help. These are hot leads that want and need my help. They have answered all my questions and qualified themselves to me. There are no surprises when I get on the phone or meet with these people. It's not cold calling, in fact, it's not sales calling. I'm simply and genuinely getting on the phone to help someone.

I am closing sales, on the phone or in person, but not by selling. Remember the formula? I'm generating clients by demonstrating that I can truly help them and then offering to help them some more. Sounds easy right? It is, but I don't do any of this off the cuff. Just like there's the seven-step process I follow to bring pull them in, there is a well-scripted four-step process I use to walk them toward becoming a client.

Step #1: Collaboration. I take the information they provided when they qualified themselves to me and ask questions that are more specific about where they are today and where they'd like to be a year from today. I also ask questions about their current leads, closing ratio and what happens to the leads they don't close. I ask about their clients, what they buy, what they spend and how often they buy. Through this process, we're starting to build a plan together. I'm not pushing any agenda on the prospect. I'm just asking questions such as, "What are you doing about this? And, "What do you think would happen if we did that?" Once I've gone through this part of the process, I have ideas about upsell strategies, back end strategies and better lead generation strategies.

Step #2: The Prescription. Once I have gathered all this information and diagnosed the situation, I get to present the prescription. Up to this point, I haven't told the prospect what to do; I have just asked questions. Now, I start prescribing activities. I usually pick three items from the plan that we collaboratively built and offer a strategy by suggesting things they could do, try or consider. I lay out a plan of action for implementation of these items. As I go through each item, I generally hear comments like, "That's a good idea," "I never considered that," or "Yep, I think that would work."

Step #3: Pre-Close. I ask a simple one sentence pre-closing question. I've basically just given back all of the answers that the prospect gave me, but created a plan of action out of them. Then I ask, "Does this sound like an effective plan to you?" If I hear anything but "Yes," it usually means there's some strategy that wasn't quite understood, so we just revisit that part of the plan and I answer every question.

Step #4: The Close. When the prospect says "Yes," then my closing question is just as simple: "Would you like me to help you implement this plan going forward?" To date, I get roughly six in ten that I talk with to say yes. I know others who are getting closer to eight or nine to say yes, but they've been at it longer and have had the opportunity to tweak their process to its optimal level. The key here is that you don't have to be a hardcore salesperson; nobody wants to be pitched at, or sold to. They just want to be helped.

If you can demonstrate your ability to help your prospects and customers by actually helping them, and then asking if they'd like more help, you can grow your business with a whole lot less aggravation and stress.

I encourage you to think about how you might implement this strategy into your business. If you're tempted to say, "But my business is different," then I challenge you to rethink that belief. It may be true that on some level, our businesses are different, but they are far more alike than you realize.

I'd like to hear about your successes and questions. Please reach out and post your stories or questions within our Facebook or Blog page community. You'll find them at https://www.facebook.com/marketingmindsetbook and http://mekamulticastmarketing.com.

Chapter Summary

Start with getting clear on your "why." Simon Sinek explains in his book that people don't buy what you do or how you do it, but why you do it. He also explains that you need to have this in mind in order to cross the chasm to get the vast majority of your niche buy your product.

If you use the Client Centric model to build your marketing message, you turn the table so your prospects qualify themselves to you. "Selling" this way means you never have to sell. Your sales conversation, instead, becomes one of:

Collaboration. You're simply ask clarifying questions about the qualifying answers they provided.

Prescribed solution. You offer your suggestions for what they can do to solve their problem.

Pre-close. You are merely asking if your prescription makes sense and more fully explaining any questions they have.

The close. The only question that remains, "Would you like me to help you implement the plan"?

Additional Resources

Below are a number of books and links to information I have referenced in this book as well as others you may find valuable as you work to implement the ideas and strategies that I've shared.

Dan Kennedy:

The MOST INCREDIBLE Free Gift Ever!

Claim your FREE gift from Dan Kennedy–*$633.91 Worth of Pure Powerful-Money Making Information.*

Go Here Now:
www.marketingmindsetbook.com/KennedyGift

Books by Dan Kennedy (Just a sampling):

No B.S. Sales Success in the New Economy

No B.S. Guide to Marketing to the Affluent

No B.S. Guide to Trust-Based Marketing

No B.S. Guide to Marketing to Leading Edge Boomers and Seniors

No B.S. Price Strategy

Marketing Mindset

Ultimate Marketing Plan

Ultimate Sales Letter

Mike Koenigs:

Books by Mike Koenigs:

Publish and Profit / *A 5-Step System for Attracting Paying Coaching and Consulting Clients, Traffic and Leads, Product Sales and Speaking Engagements*

Author Expert Marketing Machines / *The Ultimate 5-Step, Push Button, Automated System to Become the Expert, Authority and Star in Your Niche*

Make Market Launch IT / *The Ultimate Product Creation System for Turning Your Ideas into Income*

Podcast Strategies / *How to Podcast – 21 Questions Answered*

Multicast Marketing / *How to Podcast, Publish and Promote Your Content to the World with Google Hangouts, YouTube Live, Kindle Books, Mobile and Social Media*

You. Everywhere. Now. / *Get Your Message, Products and Services In Front of Your Target Prospects and in Every Pocket, Screen, Car and Television in the World with the Help of the Largest Brands*

Frank Kern:

Books by Frank Kern

Convert: *The Simple Little Formula That Sold $450 Million Worth of Products Online*

How I Created a $175,000 Per Month Consulting Business in 90 Days

Other Recommended Resources:

Glaser-Kennedy Insiders Circle
www.marketingmindsetbook.com/GKIC

Start with Why by Simon Sinek / (Book)

The Charge by Brendon Burchard / (Book)

The E-Myth Revisited by Micheal Gerber / (Book)

Uncensored Sales Strategies by Sydney Barrows (Book)

The New Money Masters by Anthony Robbins with Frank Kern (Audio CD)

Establish Yourself as a Media Expert: www.helpareporter.com

For Additional Information and Resources go to:

www.MarketingMindsetBook.com

Marketing Mindset

About the Author

With a strong blend of marketing, economics, behavioral psychology and consulting in his 35 years in business development, Mr. Klipsch is focused on getting results.

In his early days in the transportation industry, he became a leading authority in the intermodal transportation of liquid bulk products, and consulted with many Fortune 100 companies such as Dow Chemical, Procter &

Gamble, Honeywell and governmental entities such as the Department of Defense.

Since then, he has continued to deliver both strategic and technical solutions to a variety of complex business issues for international corporations such as O-I, Inc. and Diageo, but has enjoyed some of his greatest experiences working with much smaller professional services providers. Mr. Klipsch is a champion for small business and serves on the executive committee for the SCORE chapter in St. Louis, Missouri as well as supporting small businesses through his BNI network. He also supports several charitable organizations that help start businesses around the world including the Just Like My Child Foundation and The Girl Power Project. Locally, he sits on the board of directors for Caring Solutions of Greater St. Louis, an organization that helps developmentally disabled persons and their families with their behavioral, health and vocational needs.

To communicate with Mr. Klipsch directly about his availability for speaking engagements, mastermind meetings, or consulting opportunities, please fax your inquiry to (815) 828-2039, or write to MEKA Multicast Marketing at 5640-B Telegraph Road, Suite 159, St. Louis, MO 63129, or phone (314) 492-3838.

Mr. Klipsch takes calls by appointment only and uses email very discriminately.

In memory of William F. Klipsch Sr. and Jr.

www.ingramcontent.com/pod-product-compliance
Lightning Source LLC
Chambersburg PA
CBHW061738020426
42331CB00006B/1277